This

TO Brittany

Little Paw™

Little Paw is the children's imprint of Muscatello Publishing.
www.LittlePaw.com
Post Office Box 620011 Orlando, Florida 32862

Printed in the United States of America

First Edition ISBN 0-9722774-0-5 (Soft Cover)
Library of Congress Cataloging-in-Publication Data

LittleBoyLuc™

PRESENTS

Who's There?

101 Knock Knock Jokes for Kids

Luc

LUC DeTELLIS

Little Paw™

Orlando, Florida

When my daddy comes to tuck me in at bed time, we enjoy telling knock knock jokes. In this book I share with you some of the jokes we have made up during our bed time routine. Enjoy laughing, learning, and making up your own knock knock jokes too.

Remember that you can enjoy life by laughing more.

Your friend,
Luc DeTellis
Luc@LittleBoyLuc.com

Luc DeTellis

Knock knock.

Who's there?

Me.

Me who?

Me who loves you.

Knock knock.

Who's there?

Pizza.

Pizza who?

Pizza with extra cheese.

Knock knock.

Who's there?

Hurry.

Hurry who?

Hurry up, and please answer the door.

Knock knock.

Who's there?

Mary.

Mary who?

Mary who had a little lamb.

Knock knock.

Who's there?

Choo choo.

Choo choo who?

Choo choo the train.

Knock knock.

Who's there?

Tickle.

Tickle who?

Tickle you.

Knock knock.

Who's there?

Daddy.

Daddy who?

Daddy who loves you.

Knock knock.

Who's there?

I'm gonna get.

I'm gonna get who?

I'm gonna get you.

Knock knock.

Who's there?

Sippy.

Sippy who?

Sippy cup.

Knock knock.

Who's there?

The letter B.

The letter B who?

The letter B that comes after A

Knock knock.

Who's there?

Stars.

Stars who?

Stars who are up in the sky.

Knock knock.

Who's there?

Soft.

Soft who?

Soft pillow.

Knock knock.

Who's there?

Sweet.

Sweet who?

Sweet tea.

Knock knock.

Who's there?

Yummy.

Yummy who?

Yummy ice cream with sprinkles on top.

Knock knock.

Who's there?

Toasted.

Toasted who?

Toasted marshmallow.

Knock knock.

Who's there?

Tooth.

Tooth who?

Tooth brush.

Knock knock.

Who's there?

Shopping.

Shopping who?

Shopping cart.

Knock knock.

Who's there?

Chocolate.

Chocolate who?

Chocolate milk.

Knock knock.

Who's there?

Dough.

Dough who?

Dough-nut.

Knock knock.

Who's there?

Birdie.

Birdie who?

Birdie who says tweet, tweet, tweet, tweet.

Knock knock.

Who's there?

Kitty.

Kitty who?

Kitty being chased by the doggy.

Knock knock.

Who's there?

Rain.

Rain who?

Rain falling on the window.

Knock knock.

Who's there?

I.

I who?

I know you.

Knock knock.

Who's there?

Piggy.

Piggy who?

Piggy bank.

Knock knock.

Who's there?

Your.

Your who?

Your sister who wants to play with you.

Knock knock.

Who's there?

Cows go.

Cows go who?

No, cows go moo!

Knock knock.

Who's there?

Ketchup.

Ketchup who?

Ketchup to me and I will tell you.

Knock knock.

Who's there?

Interruptive dog.

Interruptive dog - WOOF, WOOF, WOOF!

Knock knock.

Who's there?

Ben.

Ben who?

Ben knocking on the door too long, please let me in.

Knock knock.

Who's there?

According.

According who?

According to the weatherman, it's going to rain tomorrow.

Knock knock.

Who's there?

Car go.

Car go who?

Car go beep, beep.

Knock knock.

Who's there?

Noodles.

Noodle who?

Noodles and cheese.

Knock knock.

Who's there?

Avenue.

Avenue who?

Avenue you heard of this joke before?

Knock knock.

Who's there?

Flash.

Flash who?

Flash light.

Knock knock.

Who's there?

Ice.

Ice who?

Ice cream.

Knock knock.

Who's there?

It's past your.

It's past your who?

It's past your bedtime, isn't it?

Knock knock.

Who's there?

Honey brush.

Honey brush who?

Honey brush your hair.

Knock knock.

Who's there?

Special.

Special who?

Special delivery.

Knock knock.

Who's there?

It's time.

It's time who?

It's time for you to wake up.

Knock knock.

Who's there?

Umm.

Umm who?

Umm I forgot.

Knock knock.

Who's there?

Santa.

Santa who?

Santa Claus and Rudolf.

Knock knock.

Who's there?

Shh.

Shh who?

Shh, quiet, the baby's sleeping.

Knock knock.

Who's there?

Bounce.

Bounce who?

Bounce the ball.

Knock knock.

Who's there?

Little boy.

Little boy who?

Little boy Luc.

Knock knock.

Who's there?

Fish.

Fish who?

Fish and chips.

Knock knock.

Who's there?

Astro.

Astro who?

Astronaut.

Knock knock.

Who's there?

Pop.

Pop who?

Pop corn.

Knock knock.

Who's there?

I'm gonna kiss.

I'm gonna kiss who?

I'm gonna kiss you.

Knock knock.

Who's there?

See.

See who?

See shell.

Knock knock.

Who's there?

I think.

I think who?

I think it's you.

Knock knock.

Who's there?

Ding dong.

Ding dong who?

Ding dong goes the door bell.

Knock knock.

Who's there?

The mail.

The mail who?

The mail man.

Knock knock.

Who's there?

Somebody.

Somebody who?

Somebody who loves you.

Knock knock.

Who's there?

Thinking about.

Thinking about who?

Thinking about you.

Knock knock.

Who's there?

I.

I who?

I love you.

Knock knock.

Who's there?

Happy birthday.

Happy birthday who?

Happy birthday to you.

Knock knock.

Who's there?

I just forgot.

I just forgot who?

I just forgot who's there.

Knock knock.

Who's there?

Somebody.

Somebody who?

Somebody who's knocking on the door.

Knock knock.

Who's there?

Doctor.

Doctor who?

Doctor makes me feel better.

Knock knock.

Who's there?

Teddy.

Teddy who?

Teddy bear.

Knock knock.

Who's there?

Pen.

Pen who?

Pen and paper.

Knock knock.

Who's there?

Rubber.

Rubber who?

Rubber ducky.

Knock knock.

Who's there?

Lemon.

Lemon who?

Lemonade.

Knock knock.

Who's there?

Vanilla.

Vanilla who?

Vanilla ice cream.

Knock knock.

Who's there?

Your.

Your who?

Your best friend.

Knock knock.

Who's there?

Pizza.

Pizza who?

Pizza delivery.

Knock knock.

Who's there?

Timmy.

Timmy who?

Timmy and Samson.

Knock knock.

Who's there?

Mr.

Mr. who?

Mr. Green Frog.

Knock knock.

Who's there?

Peanut butter.

Peanut butter who?

Peanut butter and jelly.

Knock knock.

Who's there?

My sister.

My sister who?

My sister Kate.

Knock knock.

Who's there?

One plus one.

One plus one who?

One plus one equals two.

Knock knock.

Who's there?

Organ.

Organ who?

Organizer.

Knock knock.

Who's there?

123.

123 who?

123 I'm gonna take a picture of you.

Knock knock.

Who's there?

Chess.

Chess who?

Chess-nut.

Knock knock.

Who's there?

Air.

Air who?

Airport.

Knock knock.

Who's there?

Sunny.

Sunny who?

Sunny day.

Knock knock.

Who's there?

Outside.

Outside who?

Outside here I come.

Knock knock.

Who's there?

Cover.

Cover who?

Cover me with a blanket, I'm cold.

Knock knock.

Who's there?

Boom chick.

Boom chick who?

Boom chick goes the drum.

Knock knock.

Who's there?

King

King who?

King of the bed.

Knock knock.

Who's there?

Runner.

Runner who?

Runner who ran real fast and wants
to come home and take a nap.

Knock knock.

Who's there?

Key.

Key who?

Key who unlocked the door.

Knock knock.

Who's there?

Washer.

Washer who?

Washer machine.

Knock knock.

Who's there?

Room.

Room who?

Room who needs to be cleaned.

Knock knock.

Who's there?

Funny hat.

Funny hat who?

Funny hat who looks funny on your head.

Knock knock.

Who's there?

Grandma.

Grandma who?

Grandma who lives faraway and came to visit you.

Knock knock.

Who's there?

Light.

Light who?

Light bulb.

Knock knock.

Who's there?

Vacuum.

Vacuum who?

Vacuum cleaner.

Knock knock.

Who's there?

Cry.

Cry who?

Crying boy who needs to laugh.

Knock knock.

Who's there?

Birdie.

Birdie who?

Birdie who ate the birdseed.

Knock knock.

Who's there?

Yummy root.

Yummy root who?

Yummy root beer.

Knock knock.

Who's there?

Knock knock jokes

Knock knock jokes who?

Knock knock jokes that make you laugh.

Knock knock.

Who's there?

Grilled.

Grilled who?

Grilled cheese sandwich.

Knock knock.

Who's there?

Black and white.

Black and white who?

Black and white soccer ball.

Knock knock.

Who's there?

It's time for.

It's time for who?

It's time for Luc to do a concert.

Knock knock.

Who's there?

My uncle.

My uncle who?

My uncle Zach.

Knock knock.

Who's there?

Star.

Star who?

Star fish.

Knock knock.

Who's there?

French.

French who?

French fries and ketchup.

Knock knock.

Who's there?

Orange.

Orange who?

Orange juice.

Knock knock.

Who's there?

A shoe.

A shoe who?

A shoe who needs to be tied.

Knock knock.

Who's there?

I don't know.

I don't know who?

I don't know who's there.

Who's There?

Also available by Muscatello Publishing and Little Paw:

The Adventures of
TIMMY and SAMSON

Goodbye and Hello

Written by Tim and Danika DeTellis
Illustrated by Christian Slade

Join Timmy and Samson as they discover what it means to say goodbye.
ISBN 0-9722774-0-4 (Hard Cover)
Available online at www.TimmyandSamson.com and
your favorite bookstore.